Absalom Backas Earle

Abiding peace

Absalom Backas Earle

Abiding peace

ISBN/EAN: 9783743423596

Hergestellt in Europa, USA, Kanada, Australien, Japan

Cover: Foto ©Lupo / pixelio.de

Manufactured and distributed by brebook publishing software (www.brebook.com)

Absalom Backas Earle

Abiding peace

ABIDING PEACE.

BY

Rev. A. B. EARLE, D.D.,

AUTHOR OF "THE MORNING HOUR," "BRINGING IN SHEAVES,"
"THE REST OF FAITH," ETC.

"If ye abide in me, and my words abide in you, ye shall ask what ye will, and it shall be done unto you." — JOHN xv. 7.

"Peace I leave with you, my peace I give unto you: not as the world giveth." — JOHN xiv. 27.

BOSTON:
JAMES H. EARLE, PUBLISHER,
20 HAWLEY STREET.
1880.

TO ALL

WHO ARE ENJOYING OR SEEKING

Abiding Peace,

THIS BOOK IS INSCRIBED

BY THE AUTHOR.

PREFACE.

I HAVE written this book principally in the form of questions and answers, because so many sincere inquirers desire these questions answered.

While, on the one hand, I have sought to show those who profess the deeper experience, what the fruit of holiness is, I have endeavored at the same time to point out some of the hindrances to this experience, and help those who are longing for abiding peace to find it.

I have also aimed to remove, as far as possible, objections that are in the minds of sincere Christians to this doctrine.

The Holy Spirit has so wonderfully stirred the hearts of Christians on this subject, that nothing will satisfy them but to know, as far as possible, what God has revealed in his Word about it. There is a great deal of hungering and thirsting after abiding peace in Christ. They want light; and nothing else will satisfy them. Nothing is gained by speaking or writing against this experience.

The Spirit, by producing this unrest in the hearts of God's people, indicates to them that there is a higher plane for their feet, — a better experience, that will satisfy this longing of the soul.

I have made the subject as plain and simple as possible, that all may understand my meaning; and by it find "the old paths," "and walk therein," "and find rest unto their souls."

May the Holy Spirit accompany the reading of these pages, and use them for the good of many a sad and inquiring heart, and bring them sweetly into abiding peace, is the sincere and earnest prayer of the author. A. B. E.

NEWTON, MASS., 1879.

CONTENTS.

Chapter		Page
I.	Unrest	11
II.	Is Christ our Example?	18
III.	Soul Travail	24
IV.	Should Soul Travail be Constant?	32
V.	Wardrobe and Habits	39
VI.	Unwilling to Profess	46
VII.	The Power of Temptation	49
VIII.	Watchfulness	53
IX.	Two Distinct Objects	57
X.	Should it be Spoken of?	63
XI.	Should all have it?	68

CHAPTER		PAGE
XII.	Is it Sinless?	74
XIII.	Some Hindrances	83
XIV.	Why Backslide?	91
XV.	Witnesses	97
XVI.	Accepted or Rejected	114

ABIDING PEACE.

CHAPTER I.

UNREST.

Is this feeling of unrest general, or only with a few restless ones?

PERHAPS there is no desire more general among the very best Christians, than to know how to abide in the fullness of Christ's love without interruption.

They say, "We are often on the mount of enjoyment, but cannot remain there." The struggle has been so long and fierce with them, that their Christian life has almost been a failure, so far as present happiness is concerned. They do not know how to do any better; yet this earnest longing continues. "Is there no other way to live? Must I plod on to the end, in this unsatisfying way?" They ask again and again, "Is there no rest for the soul until death?"

The very existence of this unrest, this dissatisfied feeling, produced as it must be by the Holy Spirit, is an implied evidence that there is a better experience for God's children; a higher plane for their feet; a graded road.

Letters come from every part of the country, and even from across the seas, burdened with this unrest. "Can you not send us a tract or book, or write us a letter showing us how to abide in the fullness of Christ's love without these breaks?"

The whole family of Christ seem to be stirred up on this important subject. Nothing will satisfy this hungering and thirsting among God's people, but that deep, rich experience of the abiding fullness of Christ's love, that I have called "the rest of faith." This has; this does; this will satisfy and fill the void within.

A letter from a minister — expressing this same dissatisfied feeling, this unrest, this longing for a deeper experience of Christ's love — reached me by mail this hour, which I will here insert. It is only one out of very many of the same character, that come in from all the evangelical denominations, asking for light on this subject.

SEPTEMBER 18, 1879.

DEAR BROTHER EARLE:— I have thought a good deal of writing you concerning my present experience; but why trouble you, I ask myself. And yet I am inclined to write, if for nothing else than to say, pray for me. I think I have never been really satisfied with my experience. I have enjoyed a good deal at times, — have been led to seek the blessing of holiness by the directions of those who said, "Believe you have it, and you have it." I have done so; but results, while good, were not satisfactory to me. I have been asking God for the blessing of a "clean heart." I have not the shadow of a doubt as to the ability of Christ to do the work; and I have just as fully and completely consecrated myself to God as I know how; and have been continually looking to God for the blessing. My soul much of the time has been a furnace of desire for abiding peace, and yet I have not received. I am not discouraged at all,—such a condition is better far than to be satisfied with what God is dissatisfied with. This blessing I must have. I do not wish to preach any longer without it. I am expecting it; but, oh, that he would come quickly! "Jesus, thine all-victorious love shed in my heart abroad," is the language of my soul. All I ask, Brother Earle, is that you would pray for me.

Your Brother, ———

Mrs. Edwards, wife of President Edwards, as far back as 1742, realized this same void within—this unrest, this longing for something more than to have evidence of regeneration. She felt sure that Christ must have made provisions for her to enjoy constantly what she did sometimes.

After she had sought and found abiding peace, she said, "My soul was filled and overwhelmed with light and love, and joy in the Holy Ghost, and seemed just ready to go away from the body." This exultation subsided into a heavenly calm and rest of soul in God, which was even sweeter than what preceded it.

Dr. Payson, after struggling with this same difficulty for many years, said, "Oh, that I had known this twenty years before!" That is, that he could have understood that Christ had made provisions for him to live and walk with him all the time without these distressing breaks in his religious enjoyment; that the keeping power was in Christ, by faith, and not in his own faithfulness.

Paul realized this same unrest, this same dissatisfied feeling. He saw and loved the perfect law of God; but sin in his members brought him into captivity. This distressed him, and caused him to cry out, "Oh, wretched man that I am, who shall deliver me from the body of this death!" He felt the need of some one to keep him moment by moment; something stronger than his resolutions of faithfulness. The Holy Spirit soon showed him that the keeping power was in Christ, by faith; that "what the law could not do, in that it was weak through the flesh"; what his faithfulness or friends could never do, — God had sent his Son to do. Here he embraced Christ as a keeping Saviour; not as a Saviour from hell — he had done that before. Then he could say in his own experience, "There is therefore now (not at death, not at some future time, but *now*) no condemnation to them which are in Christ Jesus, who walk not after the flesh, but after the Spirit." Here he found soul rest. "We that have believed *do* (not *shall*) enter into rest as he said." This was the "higher life"; not new life, but a higher plane of living: a deeper, satisfying experience.

This same void within, this unrest, is felt by almost every active Christian at times, unless he has already found and enjoys the abiding fullness of Christ's love. "The Holy Ghost thus signifying" that provisions are made in Christ (if we will receive them by faith) to satisfy all the longings of the soul, and give us a heaven of soul rest now. Not rest <u>from</u> toil, and labor, and pain, but <u>in</u> them all. "Great peace have they which love thy law; and nothing shall offend them."

This is the abiding peace of Christ.

CHAPTER II.

IS CHRIST OUR EXAMPLE?

Are we to take Christ for our example?

I THINK the crowning design of the Gospel is to bring every Christian into the perfect likeness of Christ. "For whom he did foreknow, he also did predestinate to be conformed to the image of his Son, that he might be the first-born among many brethren." "Christ also suffered for us, leaving us an example, that ye should follow in his steps." We see in Christ's life the fruit of holiness. It was perfect love that led him to espouse our cause; to undertake our redemption; and exchange a crown of glory for one of braided thorns, a regal robe in heaven for a scarlet robe on earth. "Christ Jesus came into the world to save sinners." Not so much to be happy, but to rescue the perishing. In every prayer, in every tear, in every pain, in every sermon, and in every effort, he seemed to aim steadily at the one great object of his mission — to save lost men.

He seldom, if ever, laughed; but often wept. Spent much time in prayer, weighed down with the burden of souls. See him all night in the mountain in prayer. On another occasion, rising long before day, he went into a solitary place to pray. When riding into Jerusalem, while the multitude around him were crying, "Hosanna," he beheld the city, and wept over it, saying, "If thou hadst known, even thou, at least in this thy day, the things which belong unto thy peace! but now they are hid from thine eyes."

Follow him to the garden now, and hear his prayer for three hours: "Father, if it be possible, let this cup pass from me," "sweating, as it were, great drops of blood." Not then making an atonement; that was made on the cross. Not afraid to die: he did not fear death; but to teach us how to pray, showing us that agonizing prayer will do what nothing else can.

In Christ's life we see how holiness or perfect love manifests itself—the fruit of perfection. Wherever holiness exists, it will lead its possessor to imitate Christ. "Except a man have the Spirit of Christ, he is none of his." Charity (which is love to God and man) goes abroad and seeks to save men. Selfishness begins at home, and remains at home. We may stand in doubt of the utility of holiness meetings that are not characterized by intensity of desire for the salvation of souls.

Many of the higher life meetings seem destitute of any burden for souls. The testimonies given are largely to tell of the joy "The Rest of Faith" has brought. Oh, that more would tell of days and nights in agonizing prayer; of wet pillows and aching hearts over lost men!

Bring Christ into our holiness meetings, and we should have a man of sorrows there, his face bathed in tears over lost men. But his tears would run over a shining face. Perfect love and perfect faith did not dry his tears, nor relieve him from soul travail. So will it be with us; the more holiness we have, the more we shall be like Christ; and the more we become like him, the more we shall travail in birth for souls,—the more we shall feel and do to save men from being lost.

When Christ was led away to be put to death, large numbers of women followed him, weeping, and, I suppose, crying to the officers not to put him to death. Jesus, turning to them, said, "Daughters of Jerusalem, weep not for me, but weep for yourselves and for your children." "For if they do these things in a green tree, what shall be done in the dry?" That is, "If I, who never sinned, find the cup of wrath so bitter, how will it be with those who deserve it all?" So, if we have dear ones out of Christ, let us weep over them, and do all we can to save them.

Can any one believe men are lost, and going to eternal death, and know that they must be born again soon or not at all, and not feel deeply for them? Ought we to claim to be Christ's children, unless we have soul travail for lost men? The best evidence of regeneration is intensity of desire for the salvation of souls.

After Paul had entered into the rest of

faith, he "warned every one night and day with tears, for three years." On another occasion, he uses a still stronger term: "I say the truth in Christ, I lie not, my conscience also bearing me witness in the Holy Ghost, that I have great heaviness and continual sorrow in my heart." This is the fruit of the Spirit. This burden for souls should be the experience of all who claim the higher experience.

CHAPTER III.

SOUL TRAVAIL.

Is soul travail in harmony with abiding peace?

WAS Christ's entire consecration, or the full surrender of his will to his Father, ever more marked than when he said, "If this cup may not pass away from me except I drink it, thy will be done"? This was the deeper experience, the working of perfect love. Never was he more lamb-like than when covered with bloody sweat. Did this disturb his sweetest rest in his Father's love?

So it will be with us: if we abide in Christ's love by faith, we shall feel as Christ did, and do as he did, as far as we can. We shall be with him on the Mount, and with equal pleasure in the garden; be with and like him, in proportion as we are holy.

> "Where'er he goes we cannot stay behind,
>   In what he does our hands shall have employ;
> Whene'er he suffers, sorrow fills our minds,
>   When he rejoices, we partake the joy."

If any one claims this rich, deep experience, and does not travail in birth for souls much of his time, and is not found often in some Gethsemane, something is wrong in his experience, and should at once be corrected.

Christ is never pleased with *worrying* pain; it is no benefit to him or his cause; but real soul travail is of much importance.

Many Christians suppose the "rest of faith," or an entire surrender of ourselves to God, would lift us above pain, and tears, and groans, for others; but it is a great mistake. It only puts us so completely into Christ's hands that the Holy Spirit can beget in us all the soul travail we can well endure.

Christ is our example in this respect. Many persons claim this deep and happy experience, and yet know but little about soul travail for others, and seldom, if ever, cry out, "Give me souls, or else I die." Paul says, "I have great heaviness and continual sorrow in my heart," and yet he was "always rejoicing." Christ's church, or bride, is the mother of his children. They are never born without soul travail on the part of his people. "As soon as Zion travailed she brought forth."

Some have supposed that the Word faithfully preached and the Holy Spirit would bring souls into the kingdom; but it is not so. Neither will faith do it, however clear and strong, without travail of soul. Neither will the highest ecstasies or joys of Christians do it. Nothing can be a substitute for pain. The Father cannot occupy the place of the bride; nor the Son, nor the Spirit, nor the angels.

"Jerusalem which is above, is free, which is the Mother of us all;" that is, all redeemed souls are born through her, and in no other way. This is a very different thing from anxiety. We may be very anxious for a revival, and labor hard for it, yet have no correct soul travail. Rachel was very anxious for children, and said, "Give me children, or else I die." But did this anxiety bring children into the world? Real agony for souls cries, "Lord, hold me up in my pain"; anxiety says, "roll pain on me." There is no selfishness in soul travail. When this state of heart has been begotten in us by the Holy Spirit, then labor and travail becomes a necessity. There is no other way by which that Christian can find relief. This is to the wicked "the unanswerable argument"; he cannot well resist it. No exercise brings us into a sweeter relation to Christ than soul travail, and no experience is sweeter than to become the mother of a redeemed soul. This is the joy of agony.

"It is from such experiences of soul travail with Christ that the Christian comes forth from the closet, endued with the divine gentleness and power of Christ, mightily to stir the hearts of those who have lost their first love, and to kindle the flame of his own soul upon theirs. It is such experiences that let us into, as it were, the very heart of Christ, impossible to fellowship in joy or work alone."

This is the place where Christ very tenderly says to his bride,—

"Child of my love, lean hard;
 Let me feel the pressure of thy pain.
 I know thy burden, child; I shaped it;
 Poised it in mine own hand; made no proportion
 In its weight to thine unaided strength.
 For, even as I laid it on, I said,
 I shall be near, and while she leans on me,
 This burden shall be mine, not hers.
 . . . . Yet nearer come, —
 Thou art not near enough; I would embrace thy
        pain,
 So I might feel my child reposing on my breast.
 Thou lovest me? I know it; doubt not, then,
 But loving me, lean hard."

Oh, the sweetness of these hours of soul travail! This is the deeper, higher, sweeter experience.

Usually these exercises are in the retired chamber of his love; in the closet or garden, away from the gaze of the world. (It is here that the tenderest love of the husband is manifested towards the mother of his children.) Never is such mutual love and tenderness felt between Christ and his redeemed ones, as when, through her travail of soul, an heir of glory is born. No wonder all the bells of heaven ring for joy over such an event. No one drinks deeper of the cup of joy and pleasure than the real mother of this heir of a crown of life. This is holiness in action; this is the higher life; the deeper experience; the rest of faith.

When "Christ came into the world to save sinners," all power in heaven and earth was given into his hands with which to accomplish this work. To do this in the best possible way, he redeemed his bride with his blood, from the curse of the law; secured her affections to himself in such a way that the love between them should be mutual; then united with her in holy marriage that she might become the mother of all his children. I think no soul has been born again and become a joint heir with Christ, except when Zion has travailed in birth for it. "This is the Lord's doings; it is marvelous in our eyes." This honor has Christ put upon the church.

Well may his spouse say, "My beloved is mine, and I am his." "Thy Maker is thine husband; the Lord of Hosts is his name, and thy Redeemer the Holy One of Israel. The God of the whole earth shall he be called."

CHAPTER IV.

SHOULD SOUL TRAVAIL BE CONSTANT?

Would soul travail be constant if we lived right?

MANY Christians wonder why they are not constantly pressed down in pain for their dear ones, until they are brought to Christ. They think the fault must be with themselves, and so accuse themselves of some great wrong.

There may be two reasons for these frequent seasons of relief from pain,—one is, nature could not endure a constant labor of soul; the body would die without seasons of rest from travail. Another reason for these changes from agony of soul to rest, and from rest to agony, is this: whenever we have this burden of soul laid upon us, we may know God is striving with those for whom we are burdened.

They may resist the Spirit, and perhaps cannot be brought in at that time, and you be relieved from all soul labor for them for weeks or months; and you find yourself drawn out in prayer for some other object. But again you are moved by the Spirit to pray for those same persons. This is evidence that the Holy Spirit is striving with them again. This may be repeated many times before they can be brought in; or they may, after all this, grieve away the Spirit and perish. "Ye do always resist the Holy Ghost." "My Spirit shall not always strive with man." There will be no more burden of soul for an individual after he has sinned away the day of grace. "There is a sin unto death; I do not say ye shall pray for it." No one can have a burden of prayer for him after that sin has been committed. If we have a real soul travail for any one, however vile, we may know they can be saved; it is not too late.

A minister kneeled down and tried to pray for a dying man, but could not utter a word. He tried and tried again, but could not speak one word in prayer for him, and the dying man passed away. God does not always mark the sin like that. But after a person has committed that sin, no Christian will have a burden of prayer for him.

He will not be depressed or cast down because he thinks he has sinned away the day of grace. He is never gloomy about it. It never shows itself in that way. The conscience is at ease; the spirits light and gay. Life was never more beautiful to him; he is a sinner let alone.

SHOULD SOUL TRAVAIL BE CONSTANT?

Many Christians are wonderfully perplexed to know why they feel so much more for lost souls at one time than at another.

At one time they are with Christ on the Mount, full of joy and ecstasy, saying, "Lord, it is good for us to be here"; at another time they are in such an agony for souls, that for a time they can hardly sleep or work. To-day they travail in birth for souls; to-morrow they are singing their sweetest notes of praise.

This is as it should be. If they enjoy the abiding fullness of Christ's love, and are led by the Spirit, these variations from pain of soul for others to songs of praise, back and forth, will be their experience through life. These changes will sweeten all the cup of their religious life, and give them perpetual sunshine in their own experience, if they understand its true meaning.

In this way they will not only be prepared to bring souls into the kingdom, but to take care of them after they are born. This is the deeper, sweeter life; it is really the interior life with Christ. It is not all singing, nor all pain of soul, but both. No one should claim the deeper experience without both of these exercises.

I love, in holiness meetings, to hear Christians tell of hours, and even days and nights, spent in real soul travail, as well as of songs of praise and great victories. True holiness will make us like Christ in every place. This is the way of holiness. Every one of Christ's children should have this experience; he will not truly represent Christ without it.

Only those who are familiar, by experience, with Gethsemane, are fully prepared to feed Christ's lambs. When two women brought a babe to Solomon, each claiming it as her own, Solomon soon found who the real mother was. The mother was not willing the babe should suffer. So no heart is as tender toward Christ's weak and erring children, as those who have travailed in birth for them; and no one so well prepared to take care of and nurse them.

Christ had his seasons of relief from pain of soul for lost men, and so will that Christian who walks the nearest to Christ. (Nature has its periods of rest, and so has grace.) Christ said, "Come ye yourselves apart into a desert place and rest awhile."

When we are totally abandoned to Christ, we shall only be burdened for souls when we are able to endure it. (No one could induce Christ to lay an ounce of burden on him more than he can bear.)

We need not fear to trust Christ entirely in this matter. Anywhere duty may call us to labor or suffer; in poverty or riches; in sickness or in health; living or dying, — still it will remain true to the end of this world. Wisdom's ways "are ways of pleasantness, and all her paths are peace." The martyr is as happy at the burning stake, as is a Christian in his own home unmolested. "As thy day so shall thy strength be." So let us "be careful for nothing"; "he careth for thee," only trust him without wavering.

CHAPTER V.

WARDROBE AND HABITS.

Will this experience affect our wardrobes, our habits, and our sources of pleasure?

I SELDOM speak to persons about dress or jewelry, believing, as I do, that the fullness of Christ's love, enjoyed as an abiding blessing, will not only regulate our sources of pleasure and habits, but our equipage.

Christ, no doubt, was neatly but plainly dressed. The Scriptures clearly teach cleanliness and neatness.

I often answer these questions by saying to the inquirer: First secure this precious experience; read your title clear; drink at the fountain of life until you can say, "My cup runneth over," until all doubt of your acceptance with Christ is gone. And then, from this new relation to your Redeemer, this new experience of his love, arrange everything to suit Christ and yourself. I think then your dress, and habits, and sources of pleasure, will be about right. Your tastes and Christ's will then harmonize. You cannot determine so well before this what you will do, or about your equipage. Things will appear different when the love of Christ fills your heart.

I found a minister at the South, of fine talents, earnestly seeking a deeper experience and an abiding fullness of Christ's love.

As we were about to kneel in prayer for this blessing, he asked what I thought about smoking tobacco (he was an inveterate smoker). I replied, "I have not come to talk about tobacco, but to pray with you." A few days after, as we were about to pray together again for the same thing, he said, —

"You did not tell me what you thought about smoking."

I answered as before. Not long after this I met him with a smiling face.

"Oh," said he, "what a blessing I have found! By the way, Brother Earle, I have put away my pipe."

The heart filled with the abiding love of Christ had shown him the inconsistency of using tobacco. So with other habits inconsistent with the deeper experience, — we very naturally give them up.

How many anxious inquirers are kept back from Christ; and how many of Christ's dear children have been kept from full consecration for fear they would have to give up some pleasure, or habit, or desired article of dress or jewelry, if they enjoyed the fullness of Christ's love.

My course has been in almost every such case, — if they know of nothing in the way, but only fear there may be, — to lead them at once to Christ, even if loaded with jewelry, or in costly apparel; urge them to make a full surrender of themselves, just as they are, to Christ; to become one with him, and be made whole by him.

And when satisfied that they are new creatures in Christ, and the joy of the Lord fills their hearts, let them, then, with this new love to Christ and his people in their hearts, arrange their dress and jewelry, and determine what sources of pleasure will please them. "As ye have received Christ Jesus the Lord, so walk ye in him;" that is, let them live in the same love and fellowship with him they had at first, only growing in grace as they learn more and more of Christ. I think, with the Holy Spirit leading them, and the love of Christ abiding in them, they will regulate their wardrobe and habits about as they should be.

Questions about places of amusement, I treat in about the same way. A beautiful illustration of this occurred in one series of meetings: A gay young lady, of fine culture, very fond of dancing, came to my room one day with this inquiry, "Do you think there is any harm in little parlor dances? When I go to New York, I play on the piano, and the children come in and dance."

I asked her if, in her opinion, those parlor dances created a desire for the ball-room? She replied, "Yes; they do. The children very soon ask to attend balls."

In reply to my inquiry, if she could dance as she then felt, she replied:

"I could not dance as I feel now; I never was so happy as now. I never enjoyed religion as I do now."

Her face was radiant with the love of Christ. I asked her if she thought she enjoyed too much religion. She thought not.

"Well," I said, "if you cannot dance when you enjoy religion as you do now, you will have to backslide and get cold before you will feel like dancing, or wish to."

I purposely left the question with which the conversation began, unanswered. She went home, and thought it over, and soon after said to me, "I have got through dancing."

I never knew a Christian enjoying the abiding fullness of Christ's love at the time, who desired to dance, or play cards, or attend theatres; he has something so much better, that these places and amusements are too insipid for him; he cannot afford to live on husks when his Father's house abounds with plenty. No matter whether it is right or wrong; he does not desire it while he has something so much better.

I should not like to say, those are not Christians who dance or attend theatres; but I never knew one who was walking sweetly with Christ, who desired it. He is so well satisfied with Christ that he does not need or desire anything else to fill the void.

> "But when we feel a Saviour's love,
> All good in him we view;
> Nor need we ever change again,
> For Christ is always new."

CHAPTER VI.

UNWILLING TO PROFESS.

Can a Christian enjoy abiding peace in Christ, and not profess it?

I THINK many have walked very sweetly with Christ, and had the abiding fullness of his love, in whose heart "there is no condemnation," who have never thought of professing it as such.

They had embraced Christ as their Redeemer, and had been forgiven. But finding themselves unable to resist the tempter's snares, had embraced Christ as a keeping Saviour, and were kept sweetly without thinking of it as separate from conversion. They had spoken of great peace and trust, and were more than willing to let every one know it.

No one could enjoy the abiding presence of the Comforter, and refuse to profess it, if the occasion required its acknowledgment. A very natural feeling when we enjoy sweet peace in believing, is to want every one to share it.

"Restore unto me the joy of thy salvation, then will I teach transgressors thy ways." David says, "I have not hid thy righteousness within my heart"; "I have declared thy faithfulness and thy salvation." To have so rich an experience of Christ's keeping power, and not want others to partake of it, seems very unnatural. Andrew's first impulse, after conversion, was to have his brother enjoy the same great blessing. "He first findeth his own brother Simon, and saith unto him, We have found the Messias." "And he brought him to Jesus." The angels did not wait until morning to tell the good news of Christ's advent into this world. It was too good not to be made known. So is the rest of faith when experienced.

I think any one enjoying the true life as an abiding blessing, will want to make it known to others, and will do it, if he thinks the occasion will admit of it. He may not speak of it as a blessing distinct from forgiveness. He may never have thought of it in that light, but will do it as soon as he perceives it. In hiding our experience from others, we grieve the Spirit, and lose the joy ourselves.

Reader, if you have the abiding presence of Christ with you, can anything afford you more comfort than to make it known to all about you, that others "may become partakers of like precious faith"? "Ye are my witnesses, saith the Lord."

CHAPTER VII.

THE POWER OF TEMPTATION.

Is the power of temptation as strong with this experience as without it?

I SUPPOSE the tempter's power is not weakened. He never knew better how to tempt fallen man than now. Never could he bring more influences to bear upon the weak Christian than at the present time; and never did Christ's children need a keeping power more than now. Spiritual wickedness never filled high places more than to-day. Christianity is dressed in almost every form. Never were there stronger temptations to sin than we find among us to-day. In the pulpit, and in the pew, oh, how many church members have fallen of late! There seems no safety for a moment, unless we are kept by a mighty power. The great flood of iniquity seems sweeping everything before it, so that the humble Christian cries out, "O, that I had in the wilderness a lodging-place of wayfaring men, that I might leave my people and go from them." How many are calling in distress, "Who shall deliver me?" "Is there any place where safety and soul rest can be found?" There is such a place for each one of us,—in Christ. "Come unto me all ye that labor and are heavy laden, and I will give you rest."

In Christ there is soul rest. He who led captivity captive is able to keep what we commit to him. Never was Satan's power exerted with more force and strength than when it was brought against Christ.

Temptation to sin found no sympathy in him. Those who abide in his love find the power of temptation broken, so that it is much easier to resist it. As temptation to intemperance is much less to one unaccustomed to alcoholic drinks than to one inflamed with rum; so to a Christian filled with the abiding fullness of Christ's love and presence,— one who is satisfied with God, temptation to sin has but little power. He finds such a satisfaction in God, such a completeness in religion, that he really does not long for anything else.

To realize Christ with us constantly, is a strong guard against sin. Besides, Christ has promised to keep him in the hour of temptation, and he believes he will do it; and he does do it.

Faith that does not waver becomes a strong shield against temptation. If our faith is weak, and our love cold, and the service of Christ does not afford us much pleasure,—temptation is much more likely to overcome us. The sheep away from the fold and shepherd, is an easier prey to the wolf. To fight the fight of faith is to trust Christ to protect us every minute. When temptation assails you, "Jesus, keep me" is breathed at once; and as there is no doubt in your mind but that he will keep you, at that minute, the power of Christ is brought at once against the tempter, and all is peace. This is the rest of faith, not of faithfulness. It is so easy to resist when Christ is near. Besides, the fullness of divine love really destroys, to a great extent, the desire for the pleasures of sin. The love of sin seems gone, when we are filled with the Spirit. Satan knows we must backslide to be strongly tempted to sin.

CHAPTER VIII.

WATCHFULNESS.

Will it not require great watchfulness to retain this true life rest? And can it be lost?

CHRIST everywhere enjoins constant watchfulness on the part of his children. "Watch and pray lest ye enter into temptation." "And what I say unto you, I say unto all, Watch."

Watchfulness, when you are filled with the Spirit, is very much like your breathing. You do not try to breathe, it is natural; it is painful not to breathe. So with a soul in harmony with God. His service is so easy, so natural, you are looking for opportunities to do good. It is your meat and drink to do his will. We do not need to be watching Satan, for fear he will get the advantage of us. We watch to know what Christ will have us do; watch to know his will; watch to see that we are relying on Christ for keeping power, and not on our watchfulness. Temptation is presented; but it has but little power over us, if abiding in the true life.

You have so committed the keeping of your soul to Christ that he fights your battles for you, while you trust all to him without doubting. "Thou wilt keep him in perfect peace whose mind is stayed on thee." Not Christ and your faithfulness, but Christ alone. So that you have two hands to work with now, instead of one.

Christ has covenanted to keep that soul in peace that trusts all to him, and you believe he will do it; if so, he does do it.

It is not a careless feeling, but a confiding one. Wherever duty calls, you go without fear, expecting to be kept, and are not disappointed.

Like the Israelite with the blood on the door-post, he trusted the promise God had made him, "I will see the blood and pass by." Although the cry of death was in every house about him, he was calm. God did not require him to remain by the door-post to show the blood, but said, "I will see it." Watchfulness becomes, as it were, trustfulness; it is easy then to watch, and pray, and trust.

I have met quite a number who say they once enjoyed this blessing, and lost it. But on a careful inquiry, I found they had been forgiven and justified freely, and were very happy and joyful for a season; but while they prayed and hoped to be kept in that sweet state of heart and life, they did not believe without a doubt that Christ would keep them there.

The difficulty was in their faith; they could not quite believe, and so Christ could not keep them. It is the rest which faith brings. "If thou canst believe;" "all things are possible to him that believeth." If legions of pure angels could sin and fall, I should not like to say we could not backslide. I mean it is possible to go back into the old plodding — up and down way of living. Yet in all the cases I have found, their faith for keeping power was deficient. If you find your unbelief is in the way, ask God to help and remove that unbelief.

I think when any one comes to believe that Christ will keep him in the abiding fullness of his love, he will not be likely to lose it.

CHAPTER IX.

TWO DISTINCT OBJECTS.

Is the faith that enables us to abide in the fullness of Christ's love, different from the faith exercised at regeneration?

"According to your faith be it unto you," will remain true until the end of time. Every one of us has, in actual possession now, just what we have believed for. "What things soever ye desire when ye pray, believe that ye receive them, and ye shall have them." "If we know that he hear us, whatsoever we ask, we know that we have the petition that we desired of him." That is, if we know that our prayer is the prayer of faith (a very difficult thing for an erring Christian to know), then we know he hears us, and we have the thing desired.

When we saw ourselves lost sinners, we embraced Christ as our Redeemer, and we received the evidence of our conversion. It was just what we believed for. We rejoiced in Christ as our Saviour from hell. We had not felt up to that time the need of one to keep us from falling. We thought our faithfulness, with God's blessing, would do that; "we thought our summer would last all the year." We wondered why every one did not enjoy the same.

But soon we began to see that sin was in our members. We renewed our vows of faithfulness; fasted and prayed, and were forgiven, but were in captivity again. And so our religious enjoyment fluctuated. To-day, happy; to-morrow, unhappy; until it was plainly shown to us that we needed more than regeneration. We needed a keeping power we did not possess. Then our cry was, "Who can do it?" "Who shall deliver me from the body of this death?" The Spirit, sooner or later, answers the earnest cry of Christ's children for light. Like Paul, we begin to say, "I thank God through Jesus Christ." Light beamed upon the mind; we now saw that God had provided in Christ a keeping power. "What the law could not do," and what our faithfulness had failed to do, God had sent his Son to do. Then we embraced Christ; not as a Saviour from hell, — we had done that before, — but as a keeping Saviour, to keep us in sweet peace moment by moment. Here also we received just what we believed for, and at once entered into soul rest in all the labors and trials of life.

Now the conditions were met by faith,

so that Christ could keep us sweetly. "He could do no mighty works there, because of their unbelief." That is, unbelief prevented the display of omnipotent power. So unwavering faith will prepare the way for that power to be exerted.

It is the same faith; faith in the same Saviour, but for two distinct blessings,— one for forgiveness of sin, the other for the abiding fullness of his love. Let us remember, then, that whatever we want of God we are to believe for that definite thing. When the Apostle James said, "The prayer of faith shall save the sick, and the Lord shall raise him up," he meant faith for that particular blessing. Whatever we can believe for without doubting, we are sure to have; it cannot fail. "Faith is the substance of things hoped for," whatever it may be. It is to its possessor what a deed of a piece of land is to its owner.

We can never believe for a thing God sees he cannot give. We can always receive an answer to the prayer of faith; but it may be a negative answer, as in the case of David for his little son, and Paul for the removal of the thorn. Faith receives the answer to prayer, and either gets the thing prayed for, or something better. If the thing prayed for cannot be granted, you will not have faith for that definite thing, only that you can be answered.

If God has clearly promised a given blessing, we may, and should, believe for that, and thus receive it. If it is promised, it is an indorsed check on the bank of heaven. If the thing we pray for can be granted, although not clearly promised, God in that case gives special faith, so that we feel sure of it from the witness of the Spirit. For instance, God has nowhere promised that a particular person will be converted, if every Christian on earth should fast and pray for him. God decreed the unfettered volition of that man's will, and cannot violate that decree. The man may resist all, and perish. Prayer avails much; and in answer to prayer, God will save him, if possible; and if we come to believe firmly that the man will be converted, it is because God sees that he will surrender all, and the Spirit communicates this special faith to us. This accounts for firm faith in one case, and no real faith in the other. Faith, then, that enables us to abide in Christ's love, and faith at regeneration, is the same, only for two different blessings.

CHAPTER X.

SHOULD IT BE SPOKEN OF?

Should this experience be spoken of everywhere?

GREAT wisdom is needed to know just when and where to introduce any subject, however dear to us, that we know is distasteful to those with whom we would speak.

To give a sick person medicine he is not prepared for, might prove very injurious, although it is just the medicine he needs. Prepare the system for it, then administer to him. There is a time to speak on every right subject, and a time to be silent. Our Saviour told his disciples, when they entered a house, "First say, Peace be to this house; and if the Son of Peace be there, your peace shall rest upon it; if not, it shall turn to you again." That is, introduce the subject of religion, and if it is an unwelcome subject to the house, you will get no hearty response. In that case, obtain a hearing some other way, if you can, and be ready at the very first opportunity to speak of Christ to them. So on this subject: ascertain, if possible, if those you wish to lead up higher are ready to hear you; if not, take more time to prepare the way. "Never ride a hobby."

There are many things in religion that Christians harmonize in; these we can speak more freely about.

If you have experienced something you think other Christians have not, and you learn they are opposed to, let them see in your spirit and life the fruit of this glorious experience. In many cases they will seek an interview with you on the subject, or the way will open for you to speak to them. Perhaps you can give them a book or tract on the subject. In any event, do not compel them to hear you often against their will, if it can be avoided. "Be ready to give to every man that asketh, a reason of the hope that is in you with meekness and fear."

I think much injury has been done, and much prejudice excited against this subject, by Christians who mean well, in almost every meeting they attend, saying in what appears a heartless manner, "I love God with all my heart, and my neighbor as myself," "Jesus saves me now," or something like this. Even if it is true, we do not need to speak of it generally, as if we had nothing else to speak of.

Let us speak of what God has done for us, and is doing, with great humility and tenderness, if we would win others to this experience.

Come oftener to meeting from the closet, to say with Paul, "I have great heaviness and continual sorrow in my heart,"—in view of the condition of lost men; or with Jeremiah, "O that my head were waters, and mine eyes a fountain of tears, that I might weep day and night for the slain of the daughter of my people"; or with Jesus, "He beheld the city, and wept over it."

Let these tears always run over a shining face, that all may see that, while Jesus keeps you sweetly in his love, yet you sorrow for others. "Sorrowful, yet always rejoicing." The fruit of holiness, or perfect love in Christ, was tears, and agony, and death itself, for lost men. If all who profess the higher or deeper experience, when they speak of resting so sweetly in Christ themselves, would at the same time satisfy the unconverted that they are "greatly concerned for their salvation," their influence on this subject would be greatly increased.

An experience that leads us to weep over lost men, and seek to lead them to Christ, can be spoken of almost anywhere with safety. "He that winneth souls is wise." Let no one shrink for a moment from confessing their experience of Christ's love. May the Holy Spirit give us wisdom to know just when and where to speak for Christ. May all who read these pages have wisdom to know when to tell what God has done for them, and courage to defend the truth on this subject as well as others.

CHAPTER XI.

SHOULD ALL HAVE IT?

Ought every Christian to have this experience?

LUKE says, Christ "commanded them (the disciples) that they should not depart from Jerusalem, but wait for the promise of the Father." This was their outfit for their work. It is not optional with us whether we will put on the whole armor of God or not. "Abide in me, and I in you." "If ye abide in me, and my words abide in you, ye shall ask what ye will, and it shall be done unto you." This is on condition that we abide in him.

Are we at liberty to do differently from this, even if we are willing? It is not our loss so much, but the cause of Christ that suffers, from our want of preparation for our work. A tree or plant, abiding in the soil, takes deep, strong root, and brings forth much fruit; but if taken out of the soil frequently, — although replaced with tender care, — will be dwarfish, and bring forth but little fruit. So with Christ's children; if they abide without interruption in the fullness of Christ's love, they will not only grow rapidly, but bring forth much fruit.

While every grace is strengthened by abiding, so every power for doing good is weakened by fluctuating. If the Father is glorified by our bringing forth much fruit, he is dishonored by our want of fruit.

To abide in the fullness of Christ's love,

gives great courage and humble boldness to his children. "When they saw the boldness of Peter and John — they took knowledge of them that they had been with Jesus."

Help is always at hand, if we abide in Christ, and he in us. "If a man love me, he will keep my words, and my Father will love him; and we (Father and Son) will come unto him, and make our abode with him." Oh, what distinguished guests to have in our homes! Then all power, all wisdom, and all possible perfections are constantly at hand. "He that dwelleth in love, dwelleth in God, and God in him." So that if we want to dwell in God, dwell in love.

Let us remember that we are bound to dwell in love. There is no choice about the matter. "It is the command of God, and therefore he is perfectly willing and anxious to make us able to do it." If your faithfulness will not secure to you abiding rest in Christ, ask Jesus to keep you in his love all the time; and if your faith is unwavering, he will keep you every moment. "What things soever ye desire when ye pray, believe that ye receive them, and ye shall have them." If you ask him in faith to give you abiding rest and peace, you will have it; you cannot fail to receive it. We are kept by the power of God, through faith.

As a soldier has no right to go to the battle-field without his armor, even if he is willing, so every Christian is required to obtain his full outfit for work. Christ "commanded them, that they (his disciples) should not depart from Jerusalem, but wait for the promise of the Father; which, saith he, ye have heard of me." This was binding on them all. Nothing could be a substitute for power from on high, — the abiding fullness of the Spirit, the rest of faith, or, as many express it, the baptism of the Holy Ghost.

What a wonderful increase of power was given to the disciples on the day of Pentecost. They could face any danger or difficulty after that. This went with them down through all their ministry, and God was greatly glorified by this increase of spiritual power.

Let me inquire of the reader, "Have you in actual possession the abiding rest of faith in Christ?" If not, will you not at once put on this important part of the Christian's armor? Not rest from labor and toil, or even suffering, if Jesus wills; but rest in them all. In this state you will not worry at things that seem dark and mysterious; but, trusting all with God, your peace will be as a river, and your power to do good greatly increased; while the wicked around you will want that peace and rest in Christ that so wonderfully sustains you in labor, in suffering, and in death.

CHAPTER XII.

IS IT SINLESS?

Is the true abiding life in Christ a sinless state?

IT has been a subject of much thought and careful inquiry with me, to know if the word of God teaches the doctrine of sinless perfection in this life. Whatever God's word teaches, I wish to practice and teach, whether I fully comprehend it all or not. I have adopted the Bible as the law of my heart and life. I do not use the expression, "sinless perfection," because I believe the Scriptures nowhere teach it as attained in this life, except in a qualified sense.

I would recommend all Christians not to use the expression. This term, "sinless perfection," caused me to hesitate about making any effort to abide without interruption or condemnation in Christ. I became satisfied that it would be the rest that faith brings, if I obtained it; and as "faith is a persuasion of the mind resting upon evidence," I must have the word of God to rest that faith upon. And as I could not find in the Scriptures the doctrine of sinless perfection in this life, I could not seek it in faith; and so I stumbled on. I found a few Christians in the different denominations, claiming this attainment. They evidently were devoted Christians walking very correctly with Christ, but did not seem perfect to me.

All this time I was much dissatisfied with my up and down experience. My own unrest increased. It is evident to me now, that the Holy Spirit was thus signifying to me that there was a better life; a higher plane; a deeper experience,—where the soul might abide in the fullness of Christ's love without interruption, no matter what might occur. I could not be happy in this unsettled state. Something must be done. I must have more than I then possessed. I saw clearly that the Bible taught something on this subject. I could find sweet soul rest taught even in this life. I collected such passages as these: "Thou wilt keep him in perfect peace whose mind is stayed on thee; because he trusteth in thee." "If ye abide in me, and my words abide in you, ye shall ask what ye will, and it shall be done unto you."

I found Enoch had walked with God for hundreds of years, and was translated to heaven without going into the grave at all.

Paul says, "There is, therefore, now (not at some future time, but *now*) no condemnation to them that are in Christ Jesus, who walk not after the flesh, but after the Spirit." Here was one living, working, and walking before God without condemnation. Then I found this same apostle, four years after, writing to the Phillipians, and saying to them, "Not as though I had already attained, either were already perfect: but I follow after, if that I may apprehend that for which also I am apprehended of Christ Jesus." In the same connection, he says, "Let us, therefore, as many as be perfect, be thus minded." I saw clearly that it was perfection in a qualified sense only.

At last, after a long search and a great struggle, I decided that the secret of abiding rest in Christ, was not by my coming into a sinless state, nor in my perfect obedience to God's law, but in being so completely in Christ, by faith, that he could have the entire control of my whole being, soul and body. Such a surrender of my will to his, that I should have nothing to say about how he should give me rest; that should be left entirely with him. No help wanted from me; Christ would give rest when, and how, and as he thought best. It was enough for me that he, with all power in heaven and earth in his hands, said, "I will give you rest." That, after letting go of everything else, and committing myself into his hands to be made whole, I should be passive, so far as helping him was concerned. Like a sick patient, after putting himself into the hands of a skillful physician, takes ether or chloroform, that there may be no struggle on his part, but trusting all to the physician. So with us; it is not Jesus and our struggles, but Jesus alone. We are to trust Christ to effect a perfect cure; to trust him just as we are in all our guilt and pollution. "All things are possible to him that believeth."

I have not called it perfect love, nor perfect faith, nor perfect anything, so far as our act is concerned, except in a qualified sense. The gospel was made for imperfect men. We embraced it with the best faith we had, in our weak, palsied condition. Here Christ met us, and took us as we were. So in giving us abiding peace. As soon as we could trust him entirely, no staggering at the promise, "I will give you rest," he did it; but in his way, not ours. He always leads the blind differently from what they plan.

At this point the reader may desire to ask a few questions:

"Does not our heavenly Father require

perfection of each one of us; and, if so, can we render it in our imperfect state?"

"Be ye therefore perfect, even as your Father which is in heaven is perfect." (Matt. v. 48.)

This divine requirement will never change or be modified. No one can enter heaven with anything short of this.

The soul that takes Christ for his Saviour, is as well prepared to meet this requirement now, as he will be at death or at the judgment. "Can man be just with God?" is the question that angels wanted to look into when it was first intimated that it could be done. How precious does Christ appear just at this point. "Who of God is made unto us wisdom, and righteousness, and sanctification, and redemption." Every claim of the perfect law of God is met here by faith in Christ.

When the perfect law of God laid its

claims before Abraham for full and perfect satisfaction, Abraham offered as the only ground of his hope the finished atonement of Christ. This was counted to him as full payment for every claim the perfect law of God brought against him. "He believed God." Faith takes what Christ has done; goes to the Father and meets the demands of the law as fully and perfectly as though we had the ability without Christ. This is salvation and rest in Christ. In this way Christ is made to those that believe, "Wisdom, righteousness, sanctification, and redemption."

The sentence of death is on all our bodies. "Dust thou art, and unto dust shalt thou return." For wise reasons the gospel does not lift this sentence from the body. The promised Comforter comes to abide with us to the end. While we live in these condemned bodies, we shall need to be kept under the blood every moment. Not in condemnation, — "there is no condemnation" to one thus kept. He has both hands to work with now, since he can trust Christ without doubting.

He now has abiding rest and peace in his work, whether in toil, and pain, and suffering (if the plan of Christ is to lead him there), or in the midst of more pleasant surroundings. He sings in the night, as well as in the day. In this state of trials, grace is given as he needs. He believes that "all things work together for good" to him.

CHAPTER XIII.

SOME HINDRANCES.

What are the hindrances to this experience?

IN giving his people great victories, God often tries their faith by delaying the answer to their prayer, or tests their loyalty to him by putting them to some trial.

Before God said, "I know Abraham,"—that is, that Abraham would obey him in anything he should ask him to do,—he had tested him severely.

He seemed to say to him: "Abraham, will you obey me in all things? Will you go anywhere, and do anything I choose to require of you, whether you see the propriety of the thing or not, leaving it altogether with me to lay out your work or trials?"

Abraham at once laid himself on the altar of obedience, without knowing anything about where the path of duty might lead. He knew God could not make a mistake, or do wrong. The spirit of obedience was in his heart. He did not say, "I will obey, if it suits me," but, "I will obey, whether I feel like it or not."

In an unmistakable voice, God said, "Take now thy son, thine only son, Isaac, whom thou lovest,— and offer him there for a burnt offering upon one of the mountains which I will tell thee of." Abraham obeyed at once; arranged the altar and bound Isaac upon it, and with a firm hand raised the knife, when God said, "Lay not thine hand upon the lad, for

SOME HINDRANCES. 85

now I know that thou fearest God." "In blessing I will bless thee, and in multiplying I will multiply thy seed as the stars."

So with us; before God will abundantly bless us, he must in some way see and know that we will obey him, whether we feel like it or not. He will not put his seal upon a man that will shrink and falter when duty leads him where, for the time, the way may be dark and the road rough. Christians do not go to heaven " on flowery beds of ease."

The principal difficulty in the way of enjoying all God has provided for us is our unbelief. Christ said to the two disciples going to Emmaus, "O fools, and slow of heart to believe all that the prophets have said."

When the disciples asked the Saviour why they could not cast the devil out of a certain boy they had tried hard to cure, Christ said, "Because of your unbelief." The Saviour himself, with "all power in heaven and earth" in his hands, could do no mighty work in a certain town, because of the unbelief he met there. What a formidable barrier is unbelief to the displays of sovereign grace! Omnipotence hindered by it! What power in unbelief! "Believe on the Lord Jesus Christ, and thou shalt be saved," is no more true than "he that believeth not shall be damned."

To come into this blessed experience, it is necessary to believe it attainable. "What things soever ye desire when ye pray, believe that ye receive them and ye shall have them." Settle this first. Let your mind become clear about it. After becoming satisfied that it is attainable, then come to Christ just as you are, expecting him to give you rest as he has promised. Do not try to feel or do like some one else. Leave all that with Christ.

If you find it difficult to believe for this blessing, bring all your power to bear against this unbelief; ask others to pray with and for you on this subject. Expect Christ to fulfill his promise, "I will give you rest," whether you perceive any change in your feelings or not. When our faith no longer "staggers at the promises," and our wills are lost in God's, he will show us his glory; then he has nothing too good to give us.

Let us not imagine that some mountain of difficulty will be met, if we trust God fully. Leave all planning for ourselves out of the question. Trust him day by day, and we shall soon sing, —

"He leadeth me, he leadeth me,
By his own hand he leadeth me."

Another hindrance to this sweet experience may be the delay of the answer to prayer.

Although your consecration may be full and complete, and your will given up to God, yet for reasons we may never know, God delays the answer, and seems not to fulfill his promise to us. This may be a real trial of our faith. We know of nothing kept back; we feel sure all is on the altar. But why does he not come? Why this long delay of soul rest? This worrying must cease before we can rest.

When the Canaanitish woman came to Jesus for her daughter, he answered her not a word for awhile. But when he saw her determined to wait and trust, he said, "O woman, great is thy faith: be it unto thee even as thou wilt." The blessing was hers from that hour. No one can tell why Christ prayed in agony three hours before the answer came.

> "God is his own interpreter,
> And he will make it plain."

Paul and Silas prayed and waited until midnight for the blessing. Christ came to the disciples the fourth watch of the night. Jacob found the blessing at the break of day.

All hindrances vanish before true faith: mountains go into the sea before it; the iron gate opens before it, "of his own accord." Before it the lame leap up and walk; the sick are raised to health; the dead are quickened into life; and "through faith we understand that the worlds were framed by the word of God." Faith connects us with God himself, and makes the resources of the Infinite ours. May these hindrances soon be removed from every

Christian's heart, that, believing, he may "enter into rest." Rest in all his labors; in all his trials and sufferings; rest when he is well, and when he is sick; rest while he lives, and when his work is done on earth; and rest in heaven forever. For "there remaineth a rest for the people of God."

CHAPTER XIV.

WHY BACKSLIDE?

If this experience is real, why have so many either fallen or backslidden?

MUST a cause necessarily be wrong, if some of its advocates turn from it? Was heaven an unholy place because legions of pure spirits sinned and fell? Do men object to a home in heaven on that account? Do they say it cannot be a place of purity, or angels would not have forsaken it? Although so many church members, once active in the prayer meeting and in places of trust, have fallen, and many of them are in prison for crime, should we forsake the church and ignore her ordinances on that account? Look at the ministry. How many of them have gone out of the pulpit into prison for crime. Should the pulpit be closed on that account, and all God's ministers be proclaimed hypocrites? Was the fact that one of Christ's apostles was a thief, and joined Christ's enemies, betrayed and sold him for a small sum, a reason why the others should "also go away"? Is the rest of faith less a reality, because some of its advocates have stumbled and fallen? Or because there are marked inconsistencies among many who profess holiness?

Must we infer that the prodigal son had an unpleasant home, because he left it and lived with vile companions?

These failures only prove the possibility of forsaking the right, and pursuing the wrong.

Do these reasons prove that this rich

experience is a fiction, and should be rejected as unsound and unsafe?

Will any one speak against the higher life or abiding rest in Christ, because some of its advocates have proved that they were not in possession of this great blessing by their inconsistent lives? The tree must be known by its fruit. Love will produce love; holiness will produce holiness; hatred will bring forth its fruit.

I am very sorry to find many who claim this rich experience, manifesting a harsh, censorious, fault-finding spirit; and in some instances their lives are a reproach to religion. In this way Christ is dishonored, and many anxious Christians who long for a higher plane of living, are hindered and kept back. And yet, should they be kept back from seeking and professing this experience, any more than from making a profession of hope in Christ at all?

Any Christian sweetly resting in Christ, by faith, will have great patience; he will not be offended at every little thing. He will speak kindly, even to those he thinks are wrong. "Charity (which is love to God and man) suffereth long, and is kind; is not easily provoked; beareth all things. Charity never faileth."

There is a keeping power in the abiding fullness of Christ. You are less likely to wander and backslide, if filled with the Spirit. Peace and joy in Christ is so great, that you do not care for other things as you do in a lukewarm state. Prayer is a different exercise. The Bible is a different book. The pleasures of sin in that state are too insipid. You cannot afford to live on husks, when you have the rich provisions of the gospel. I think very few of those who have experienced the abiding fullness of Christ ever backslide.

It is very difficult to distinguish between a movement produced upon the mere animal feelings or emotions, and true holiness. How many become very happy in a good meeting, and make vows of faithfulness, and yet in a few hours are angry, or in a short time have, in a great measure, lost those joyful emotions. In Christ's day the stony-ground hearers, "anon with joy," received the word. It does not follow that we are Christians because we are very joyful; nor that we are not Christians, because we mourn. Christ says, "If ye continue in my word, then are ye my disciples indeed." The best and only safe proof of discipleship is to continue to delight in Christ's service. And the proof of holiness is holiness, or to bear the fruit of holiness.

If Moses, the meekest man,—one who had such wonderful power with God, the man through whom God revealed so much of his word to this world,—could so far forget God as to become angry, and speak so unadvisedly, that, in view of this wrong act, he could not lead Israel into Canaan; may not those who have had even a rich experience of abiding rest and faith, so far wander as to lose their first love, or even have their faith shaken? Yet would this be an argument against the doctrine of abiding rest in Christ?

We are saved at first by "believing on the Lord Jesus Christ. We enter into rest by believing for this blessing. And we are kept by the power of God through faith.

> "Faith is the bright triumphal arch
> Through which the saints to glory march."

CHAPTER XV.

WITNESSES.

Are there many witnesses to this experience?

I WILL only give the testimony of a few out of the many who profess this deep experience. Some of these enjoyed for years the abiding fullness of Christ's love, and died as they lived, still resting in Christ, by faith. Others are still abiding in this rich experience, enjoying more and more of the divine love each day, deeply regretting that they had not known the way sooner.

Rev. T. W. Greene.

"I was enabled to lay my soul and

body, time, education, and hopes, my will, my all, upon the altar that sanctifieth the gift, and believe that the offering was accepted.

"Oh, how those fifteen years of religious profession, and three years of ministerial life, seemed to be almost in vain! The blessed Jesus became mine in a fuller sense than I ever supposed it possible in this life. From that hour, a simple faith took hold of him as a Saviour mighty to save, even unto the uttermost. Oh, this is salvation, indeed! What a glorious growth in Christ I might have had, if I had received this great salvation before! I shall never cease to praise God for this blessed deliverance.

"After I was enabled to trust Jesus as a complete Saviour, I was strongly tempted that I had nothing more than I had enjoyed before, and that I ought not to speak of it as anything special; so I prayed to God to give me an experience that I could not doubt, and that the enemy even might not gainsay.

"On the 8th of January, 1866, while conversing with a minister of our place, on simple faith, the 'Holy Ghost' came upon me in mighty power. For more than an hour I was so filled with a sense of the presence of the Holy Ghost, I could hardly bear to hear anything spoken but the name and praises of the third person of the adorable trinity. Then came the precious Saviour and supped with me. I had never seen him before as he appeared then. His love melted me till I wept aloud.

"The Father and Holy Spirit were not thought of. Finally, came a consciousness of the Father's love. So it was: first the Spirit, then the Son, and lastly, the Father manifested himself unto me as he does not unto the world. How can I praise him sufficiently!" Oh, blessed three in one!

This experience with many continues through life; it should be so with all. God has said, "The path of the just is as a shining light, that shineth more and more (not less and less) unto the perfect day." So that with every redeemed soul each succeeding day should be better than the past; and it is so with every one who abides in the fullness of Christ's love. He forgets, in a sense, the things that are behind, in the constant fullness of love and wisdom that opens continually to his view; and yet "always more to follow."

Rev. Charles Fitch.

"To the praise of my Redeemer I can testify that he keeps me in that state day by day (referring to the remarks of Payson); and that I could not better describe to you the blessedness which my soul finds in Christ, than in Payson's language: 'Christ did appear to me as a sun that had spread himself abroad until the whole firmament became one glorious luminary; not darting forth rays of fire to scorch and burn me, but shedding beams of loveliness and bliss, of which my soul was permitted to drink, as from an ocean of pure, and perfect, and soul-satisfying delight.'"

Merle D'Aubigné.

"We were studying the Epistle to the Ephesians, and had got to the end of the third chapter. When we read the last two verses, 'Now unto him that is able to do exceeding abundantly above all that we ask or think, according to the power that worketh in us,' this expression fell upon my soul as a revelation from God. 'He can do by his power,' I said to myself, 'above all that we ask; above all, even, that we think; nay, exceeding abundantly above all.'

"A full trust in Christ for the work to be done in my poor heart now filled my soul."

As the company then with him all knelt together and prayed, he says, "When I arose, I felt as if my wings had been renewed as the wings of eagles. All my doubts were removed, my anguish was quelled, and the Lord extended peace to me, as a river. Then I could 'comprehend with all saints what is the breadth, and depth, and length, and height; and know the love of Christ which passeth knowledge.' Then was I able to say, 'Return unto thy rest, O my soul, for the Lord hath dealt bountifully with thee.'"

This experience wonderfully opens the Scriptures to the mind. "Then opened he their understanding, that they might understand the Scriptures." It is the work of the Holy Spirit to take the things of Christ, and show them to his children. If D'Aubigné had known how to abide, by faith, in Christ, he would have enjoyed this all the time.

Rev. Elihu Gunn.

"After many months of fruitless struggles, I at length grew weary and discouraged, and at times nearly gave up the idea that the attainment of perfect love is possible, though I never for one moment lost the conviction that a high and holy consecration to Jesus; a state of grace far different from anything I had ever experienced, was eminently practicable; nay, a most solemn duty.

"I said, 'Now is God's time for me. I will examine this question anew, and become fully satisfied in my own mind as to what is truth on this subject.' I read 'Faith and its Effects,' and other good books, and especially, with much earnestness, the Bible; and I conversed with dear Christian friends, whose kindness and prayers for me will ever be held in grateful remembrance. I could not remain long in doubt. I said, 'This is God's truth; it cannot be gainsaid. The Scripture testimony is conclusive.'

"Then another decision followed in my own mind, just as clear, and just as emphatic: 'This blessing is for all. It is for me. By the grace of God I will have it.' I sought it with my whole heart.

"Monday, June 9, 1862, memorable day in the calendar of my being, I had observed as a day of fasting and prayer. I felt happy. I felt sure of the blessing ere long, because God had promised it.

"I came into my room at night, having spent the afternoon in pastoral visiting, and immediately kneeled down to pray. I seemed at once to be wrought upon by some power out of myself, to make, then and there, that full surrender of myself to God. The whisper of unbelief was, 'I cannot do it.' But it was at once suggested, 'It must be done some time; why not now?'

"And so, almost before I was aware of it, my soul was struggling in the mighty effort to make, then and there, a vow of consecration to God which should include my whole being, and which should be irrevocable and eternal. I thought I would write this vow in my journal, and I seized my pen for that purpose, when a passage of Scripture came flashing into my mind.

I found it by the help of the concordance (I shall never want a concordance to find it again), and read, 'Of him are ye in Christ Jesus, who of God is made unto us wisdom, and righteousness, and sanctification, and redemption.' I read it over and over with amazement. 'Can it be,' I said, 'that I have read this over so many times, and never saw what was in it before! Why, if Jesus is all these things to me, then surely he is everything. He is all in all; all I need; all I want;' and I could have shouted his praise aloud. I felt that truly I had found what I had been so long seeking for; that my soul was clear across the Jordan, and in the Canaan of rest. Peace flowed into my soul like a river,—peace which nothing could disturb. It was indeed a glorious change. Preaching was now a new work to me, and has been blessed by God ever since. My confidence in him is stronger than ever. My vows are all renewed, and my sacrifice is lying on the altar, by the grace of God never to be removed."

Rev. W. H. Williams.

"While a member of the Theological Seminary, at Princeton, I was often urged and attracted by the thrilling appeal of that earnest and holy man, Dr. Archibald Alexander, and by the conversation and prayers of James Brainard Taylor, whose countenance seemed to shine by reason of the joy and fervor of his soul. Since then, I have been privileged to mingle in precious converse and sympathy with many whom I have loved and honored, and almost envied as consistent witnesses of the doctrine of a full, a present salvation.

"Early one morning, in my daily reading

of the New Testament, my eye and my heart were happily fastened upon the simple story of the leper, vile and unclean, who came and worshiped Christ, saying, 'Lord, if thou wilt, thou canst make me clean.' The words seemed at once revealed and applied by the blessed Spirit, as the full and perfect utterance of my soul. I read, 'And Jesus put forth his hand and touched him, saying, "I will; be thou clean."' My heart was touched as by that hand of power and love. Filled with gushing and overwhelming tenderness and gratitude, I rejoiced in the blessed assurance that the experience of the poor, polluted leper was mine. 'And immediately his leprosy was cleansed.'

"I have since then joyfully embraced proper occasions to confess to my brethren in the ministry and others, the full power and grace of Jesus Christ to redeem from all iniquity,—to deliver and keep me from this evil world."

Rev. Alfred Cookman.

"Frequently I felt to yield myself to God and pray for the grace of entire sanctification; but then the experience would lift itself in my view as a mountain of glory, and I would say, 'It is not for me.' I could not possibly scale that shining summit; and if I might, my besetments and trials are such, I could not successfully maintain so lofty a position.

"But some one will say, 'Had you not dedicated yourself to God at the time of your conversion?' I answer, yes; but with this difference: then I brought to the Lord Jesus powers dead in trespasses and sins; now I would consecrate powers permeated with the new life of regeneration; I would present myself 'a living sacrifice.'

Then I gave myself away; but now, with the increased illumination of the Spirit, I felt that my surrender was more intelligent, specific, and careful,—it was my hands, my feet, my senses, my attributes of mind and heart, my hours, my energies, my reputation, my kindred, my worldly substance, my everything. Then I was anxious respecting pardon; but now my desire and faith compassed more; I wanted the conscious presence of the Sanctifier in my heart.

"Do you ask what was the immediate effort? I answer, peace,—a broad, deep, satisfying, and sacred peace. This proceeded not only from the testimony of a good conscience before God, but likewise from the presence and operation of the Spirit in my heart. Still I could not say I was entirely sanctified, except as I had sanctified or set apart myself unto God.

A little while after, it was proposed that we spend a season in prayer. And while thus engaged, God for Christ's sake gave me the Holy Spirit as I had never received it (him) before. Need I say that this experience of sanctification inaugurated a new epoch in my religious life?

"Oh, what blessed rest in Jesus! What an abiding experience of purity through the blood of the Lamb! What a conscious union and constant communion with God! What increased power to do or suffer the will of my Father in heaven! What delight in the Master's service! What fear to grieve the infinitely Holy Spirit! What love for, and desire to be with, the entirely sanctified! What joy in religious conversation! What confidence in prayer! What illumination in the perusal of the Sacred Word! What increased unction in the performance of public duties!"

It is not surprising that dear Brother Cookman, who had lived and walked with Christ so many years, and enjoyed his abiding presence so uninterruptedly, should so nearly experience Enoch's translation, and utter as his last and dying words, —

> "Burst are all my prison bars,
> And I soar beyond the stars;
> To my Father's house,
> The bright and blest estate.
> Lo! the morn eternal breaks,
> And the song immortal wakes,
> Robed in whiteness
> I am sweeping through the gates."

In these experiences we see, first a longing desire for something more than to know they have been converted: a hungering after the abiding fullness of Christ's love. They generally meet some hindrances; but when all was laid on the altar, and they could believe, — not barely that Jesus was able and willing to keep them in this sweet, uninterrupted peace and rest, but that he would do it, — then they, without an exception, found rest.

Some, like Payson, have a very rich experience of the love of God, but lack the needed faith to <u>retain</u> it, and so they fluctuate in their peace and rest. Christ can so help our unbelief that we can believe without wavering; then, and not till then, we shall abide in Christ's love. Let us remember we all have in actual possession everything we have believed for. It will always be to us "according to our faith."

CHAPTER XVI.

ACCEPTED OR REJECTED.

What shall be done with this evidence?

WHEN sufficient evidence is given to establish a given truth, and men will not receive it, then the person rejecting this evidence becomes the guilty party. "If I had not come and spoken unto them, they had not had sin: but now they have no cloak (excuse) for their sin." Our responsibility is in proportion to the light we have, or might have had.

No doubt there are many mistakes and errors among the advocates of abiding peace and rest in Christ. Much we could wish were otherwise; much to regret.

But was there ever a cause free from the same charge? "Who can know his errors?"

But many rich things have been said and written on this subject. Many whose lives and education have never been called in question, testify to a deep, rich experience of the abiding peace of Christ, that removes this unrest, and satisfies this longing. All agree that "the half was never told."

Let me ask the reader to review with me these chapters, and weigh carefully these truths, and decide for yourself what you will do with the evidence.

Is not your own experience of unrest, your hungering and thirsting, expressed in these chapters? Think how often you have wished that in some way you could enjoy peace and rest in Christ without these sad interruptions.

You have made vows of faithfulness, but have not kept them. Sin in your members has led you into captivity. How many times you have asked, "Is there no other way? Must I plod on until death, in this unsatisfying way?" Have you not sometimes wondered if Christ had not made provisions for you to abide in the fullness of his love without these breaks? It was the blessed Holy Spirit who stirred up these inquiries, and caused this unrest, that he might lead you "up higher,"—up where the sun shines without interruption, that your feet might walk on the "King's highway" of holiness.

This longing for a higher plane of spiritual life, produced by the Holy Spirit, is evidence that there is a place of abiding peace and rest. As the Spirit and the Word agree, the Word must teach the doctrine of abiding peace.

I have shown you from Christ's example, that tears, and groans, and soul travail are in harmony with the sweetest rest in our Father's love; that all the pain and travail produced in our hearts by the Holy Ghost, is a pleasant exercise — "the joy of agony." Travail of soul that brings into Christ's family an heir of glory, is really the sweetest pleasure a Christian can have. It is in harmony with the word of God, and an unbroken peace.

I have shown you also that this travail of soul must be periodical, if it comes from God. The sweetest experience is not all singing, nor all pain, but both. To-day you are in travail of soul; to-morrow you are singing your sweetest notes of praise, free from pain.

This will be your experience through life, if you walk correctly with Christ.

I think, also, I have satisfied you that

professed holiness, if it does not affect our wardrobes, our habits, and our sources of pleasure, cannot be from God; that the abiding fullness of Christ's love will so satisfy this longing for something new, that really the soul does not want the pleasures of sin; that our wardrobes will satisfy those who know us; that we have found in this experience something better than jewelry or display in dress.

We have also shown in these chapters that it is possible to have this experience and not profess it. It may not have occurred to the individual to speak of it as separate from conversion, but that no one could retain it who was unwilling to profess it. Also, that this experience weakens the power of temptation to sin, in that it is so far superior to anything else; and that to go into sin, we must first backslide from Christ. Watchfulness, too, is so natural, so easy, in this state; much like our breathing; as it is painful not to breathe, so it is painful not to work for souls.

These reasons must have some weight with the reader in recommending this experience to him. Will you not say, at least, I will pray over these reasons, and open my heart to them? If God requires this experience as your outfit for his service, you cannot ignore it without divine disapprobation. He commanded his disciples not to depart from Jerusalem until they were endued with power from on high. So with us; whatever increases our power for doing good, is our duty to possess. We may not neglect it without sin.

Hindrances in the way of this experience have been removed, making the way plain, I trust, to come into abiding peace in Christ. Because some have backslidden or fallen who have advocated this doctrine, is no objection to the doctrine itself. I have also called your attention to a few out of the many witnesses, who have given a full, clear, positive experience of the abiding fullness of Christ's love. God's children are his witnesses. As we are under the dispensation of the Holy Spirit, he calls these witnesses forward when he needs them, and through them speaks to the world on this subject. This testimony is used for the benefit of others. We wish you carefully to weigh it, remembering God sent it.

I have also shown that faith in Christ for abiding peace, is the same exercised at regeneration, but for a different blessing. The higher life is not a new life, but a higher plane of spiritual living; a fuller development of the true Christian life.

In this experience, and making it known, I have endeavored to guard all against "riding a hobby." Not always to be speaking of this particular part of your experience; but to "be ready to give to every man that asketh, a reason of the hope that is in you."

I have shown, as clearly as possible, that the true abiding life in Christ is not necessarily a sinless state; but that an imperfect Christian, covered with the blood of Christ, may be kept moment by moment without condemnation.

As no doubt many will read this book who never saw the author; and many, I trust, will read it after he has gone to his account, let me speak a few closing words to each reader, separately.

Do you not desire to do the greatest amount of good possible while living? Do you not desire the very best preparation you can have to lead others to Christ?

If so, can anything give you more power than to abide in Christ? If the disciples needed to tarry ten days at Jerusalem for power from on high, after they had received power over all devils, do we not need a similar outfit?

Christ says, "He that abideth in me, and I in him, the same bringeth forth much fruit." "Herein is my Father glorified that ye bear much fruit; so shall ye be my disciples."

If the abiding fullness of Christ's love will increase our power for doing good, is not this a sufficient reason for our securing it at once? Souls are perishing all about us. Let us, therefore, take to ourselves the whole Christian armor, and do what we can.

Our personal happiness, also, is greatly increased by the abiding presence of the Comforter. There is no source of real earthly pleasure but what is made brighter and sweeter by being filled with the divine Spirit. Christ's blood removes just what is sinful, nothing else.

> "Religion never was designed
> To make our pleasures less."

"Godliness is profitable unto all things having promise of the life that now is, and of that which is to come." In this state, the little ills of life do not disturb us, as when we are lukewarm.

Oh, the joy of living where you can, as it were, daily hear the music of the harps of God, and the songs of the redeemed? "And I heard a voice from heaven, as the voice of many waters, and as the voice of a great thunder: and I heard the voice of harpers harping with their harps: and they sung as it were a new song before the throne." The scene was laid in heaven, but John heard it on earth.

Dr. Payson once, standing on the "King's highway" (where every Christian should live), said, "The celestial city is full in my view; its glories beam upon me..... Its sounds strike upon my ears." His soul seemed to cry out, —

> "Oh, for a thousand tongues
> To sing my dear Redeemer's praise!"

"A single heart and a single tongue seem altogether inadequate to my wants; I want a whole heart for every separate emotion; and a whole tongue to express that emotion."

Many of God's children have been lifted to these beautiful heights, where they could, by faith, see the King in his beauty; where the sunbeams of glory were shining all about them; where there seemed but a step between them and the inner temple, — the dwelling-place of the eternal. Then they said, —

> "My willing soul would stay
> In such a frame as this."

But for the want of abiding faith in the keeping power of Christ, they were driven back into darkness again.

Oh! that Christians would learn how to embrace Christ as a keeping Saviour, and thus abide in the fullness of his love until he shall call them to their many-mansioned home; to hear the "Well done, good and faithful servant."

Here I must close, and lay down my pen, and with an earnest prayer commit this imperfect service for Christ and his people, in connection with these pages, to the keeping of our heavenly Father. My sincere desire is, that in the day when the

Saviour's jewels are made up, it may then appear that some precious souls were enabled by it to find "Abiding Peace."

"To God only wise be glory through Jesus Christ, for ever, Amen."

By Rev. A. B. Earle, D.D.

THE MORNING HOUR. For family devotions, and private meditation. Contains a portion of Scripture, with suggestive spiritual Exposition, and a brief Hymn for every day of the year. Elegant octavo volume. Cloth, $2.00; half Leather, $3.00; full Turkey, $5.00.

"It is superior to either Jay's 'Morning and Evening Exercises' or Spurgeon's 'Morning by Morning.'" — *Central Baptist, St. Louis.*

"Its comments are everywhere full of the marrow of the gospel." — *Congregationalist, Boston.*

BRINGING IN SHEAVES. The outgrowth of the author's long experience in gospel work. 12mo. Cloth. With Steel Portrait. $1.50.

"One of the most remarkable books ever given to the public." — *Western Recorder, Louisville.*

THE REST OF FAITH. Shows how the soul may abide in sweet and constant rest in all the care of the daily life. Cloth, 50 cents; gilt edges, 75 cents; full Russia, $1.00.

"Meets the deep longings of the hungry soul." — *Watchman and Reflector, Boston.*

ABIDING PEACE. Has been written in response to the urgent need of a work to meet the difficulties that have arisen, and the objections that have been made to the doctrine of perfect deliverance from unrest and condemnation, and to enable the longing Christian to enjoy abiding peace in the daily life. 18mo. Cloth, 50 cents.

"It seems safe to say that not for years has so important a book appeared on this topic." — *The Contributor, Boston.*

THE TITLE EXAMINED; or, How May I Know I am a Christian? A book for inquirers, and for every Christian who would be sure of his title to heaven. 18mo. Cloth, 30 cents; paper, 15 cents.

"Just what one wants to have in the pocket." — *Zion's Herald, Boston.*

REVIVAL HYMNS. Contains those hymns, with the addition of a few tunes, suited to give power to the singing, in seasons of special religious effort. Large type and convenient size. Cloth, 30 cts.; paper, 15 cts. 8vo, leather, $1.00.

WHY NOT NOW? A searching tract for the careless and the anxious. 4 cents; 25 cents per dozen; $1.50 per hundred.

GROWING, BECAUSE ABIDING. Answers four important questions in regard to the rest of faith. 4 cents; 25 cents per dozen; $1.50 per hundred.

TEN EVIDENCES OF CONVERSION, with Ten Questions for Self-Examination. 10 cts. per doz.; 75 cts. per hundred.

⁎ *Any of the above works mailed postpaid on receipt of price. Descriptive catalogue of our publications mailed free.*

JAMES H. EARLE, Publisher,
20 Hawley Street, Boston, Mass.

THE CONTRIBUTOR:

A Large, Undenominational, Religious and Family Monthly, For the Home and Sunday School; For All Classes; For Old and Young.

THE CONTRIBUTOR aims to meet the want among intelligent and advanced Christians, for religious and family reading of the highest standard and most practical character, and to furnish Sunday-school teachers and scholars with the very best helps and expositions. The Sunday-school matter alone, in a single copy, makes fifty pages of a 12mo book, and is pronounced unsurpassed.

Among the writers in its columns, may be mentioned,—

Prof. WM. M. BARBOUR, D.D., A. B. EARLE, D.D., ANNA SHIPTON, DANIEL STEELE, D.D., Rev. GEORGE F. PENTECOST, Prof. O. S. STEARNS, D.D., E. F. BURR, D.D., Rev. E. P. HAMMOND, Rev. EDWARD A. RAND, Miss FRANCES E. WILLARD, and others.

WHAT IS SAID OF THE PAPER.

"THE CONTRIBUTOR is one of the freshest and best of the purely religious papers that comes to our office." — *Zion's Herald, Boston.*

"THE CONTRIBUTOR is one of the most ably-edited religious journals in the country." — *Meriden Republican.*

"THE CONTRIBUTOR knows how to be religious without being dull." — *Christian at Work, New York.*

"I cannot get along without THE CONTRIBUTOR'S Sunday-school Commentary."
WM. M. F. ROUND,
Author of "Achsah," &c.

"I wish I could put it into every Sunday-school in the land."
COL. R. H. CONWELL,
Leader of the Union Bible Class, Boston.

"THE CONTRIBUTOR I always recommend as our *best* religious paper."
REV. ELIAS NASON,
Author of "Lives of Moody and Sankey," &c.

GALFSBURG, ILL.
"I take over thirty periodicals, and rank THE CONTRIBUTOR among the *very best*."
REV. S. W. BROWN.

TERMS: $1.00 A YEAR.

Postage prepaid by the publisher. Subscriptions can begin at any time.

JAMES H. EARLE, PUBLISHER,
20 HAWLEY STREET, BOSTON, MASS.